I0159278

REJOICING IN THE LORD
A STUDY OF PHILIPPIANS

GARY C. HAMPTON

© 2016 by Gary C. Hampton

All rights reserved. No part of this publication may be reproduced, stored in a re-trieval system, or transmitted in any form or by any means without the prior written permission of the author. The only exception is brief quotations in printed reviews.

ISBN-10: 0615982840
ISBN-13: 978-0615982847

Published by Start2Finish Books
PO Box 660675 #54705
Dallas, TX 75266-0675
www.start2finish.org

Printed in the United States of America

Unless otherwise noted, all Scripture quotations are from the *New King James Version*. Copyright © 1979, 1980, 1982 by Thomas Nelson, Inc. Used by permission. All rights reserved.

Cover Design: Josh Feit, Evangela.com

CONTENTS

1

PAUL & PHILIPPI

PHILIPPIANS 1:1-2

PAUL, THE AUTHOR OF PHILIPPIANS

Paul wrote the Philippian letter from Rome during his first imprisonment. Timothy was with him at the time, so he was mentioned by Paul. The apostle probably used Timothy's name here because he was with him when the church at Philippi was started. He described both of them as servants of Christ, or we might say in bondage to Christ. It is important to realize all who have reached an age of knowing right from wrong are slaves (Rom. 6:16-18). All Christians are like slaves who have been purchased by the Lord, our master (1 Cor. 6:19-20).

Concerning the writing of this letter, Lipscomb says:

> This epistle was written by Paul while in "bonds" in the Praetorium (1:7-13.) He sends greetings from Caesar's household (4:21); he expresses expectation of some crises in his imprisonment (1:20-26); and confident hope of visiting Philippi (1:26; 2:24.) All

those indications place it in the first imprisonment of Paul in Rome which we know to have lasted "two whole years" (Acts 28:30), which certainly began in the year A.D. 61. Therefore, its date must be somewhere towards the end of the imprisonment, in the year of A.D. 63.

TO THE SAINTS IN PHILIPPI

Paul wrote to the saints, who would not be just those who were especially holy or had died in the Lord. Instead, it would include all those who were separated from sin and dedicated to God's service (1 Cor. 6:9-11). Every Christian would be included in this designation (2 Thess. 1:10).

The letter is also addressed to the bishops and deacons. It was Paul's practice, at the end of the first missionary journey, to ordain elders in every church (Acts 14:23). These men were the overseers, or bishops, of the church and were to watch for the safety of the members' souls (Acts 20:17, 28-32; Tit. 1:5-14; Heb. 13:7, 17; 1 Pet. 5:14).

All Christians are deacons or servants, but here the word is used more specifically for the office of deacon (1 Tim. 3:8-13). Their job appears to have been to attend to physical needs of the brethren and routine requirements. In doing this, they freed the elders for the more important tasks of prayer and study. Thereby they could more readily keep themselves and the flock safe (cf. Acts 6:17).

THE CITY OF PHILIPPI

D. Edmond Heibert, in his book *An Introduction to the Pauline Epistles*, gives us a little insight into the nature of the city of Philippi. "It was an inland town and was situated about eleven miles north of the seaport of Neapolis." It was strategically important because it stood at the place where a mountain pass ran through the Balkans.

The ancient name of the town was Crenides, which means, "The Little Fountains." This likely came from the number of springs in the area. Philippi II of Macedonia saw the importance of its location and took it over to protect Macedonia from the Thracians. In 356 B.C., he had it enlarged, fortified, and renamed "Philippi."

The Romans built the Via Egratia, a highway, through the pass, therefore through Philippi. In 42 B.C., the Roman Republican armies, led by Brutus and Cassius, were defeated by the armies of Mark Anthony and Octavian, who was later called Augustus. The pride brought on by the victory led Octavian to elevate the city to colony status. Its citizens were Roman citizens, and their names were enrolled in Rome's annuls. They did not have to pay poll and property tax. They were not ruled by a provincial governor, and they had the right to own land. Hiebert says the population of the city included the Roman colonists, Macedonians, and Orientals. Few Jews settled there because it was an agricultural and military city.

PAUL & PHILIPPI

Paul first visited Philippi on his second missionary journey (Acts 16). Timothy had joined Paul for the first time at Lystra. The Holy Spirit would not allow them to go to Asia or Bithynia. Instead, at Troas, Paul had a vision of a Macedonian man calling for them to come over and help them. As they set sail from Troas, Luke's account changes from a discussion of what Paul, or "he," did to what "we" did. Therefore, we conclude he joined Paul and Timothy at Troas (Acts 16:10). Immediately after receiving the Macedonian call, they sailed to Neapolis and journeyed on to Philippi, which Luke calls the chief city. We do not really know what made him say it was the chief city.

The few Jews who lived there did not have a synagogue, but they did have a place outside of the city for prayer. On the Sabbath, Paul went to that place and spoke to the women assembled there. Lydia and her household were baptized. Paul healed a damsel possessed with a spirit. He and Silas were caught, dragged to the marketplace, and beaten for it. It was in prison that they met, taught, and baptized the Philippian jailer and his household.

The magistrates wanted Paul and Silas released the next day. Paul would not be released privately, but appealed to his Roman citizenship and the fact that he was beaten without being charged. The magistrates had to go in person and ask them to leave. Hiebert thinks Paul's insistence upon his rights as a Roman citizen was very important. He says the magistrates needed to realize that this was not some insignificant revolutionary movement, as had been charged, but was being preached by Roman citizens. He thinks this may have saved the young church some later problems. After meeting with and comforting the brethren at Lydia's house, Paul and his company departed.

THE CHURCH IN PHILIPPI

It should be remembered that this group of Christians would have been included in those Macedonia Christians Paul commended for their liberality (2 Cor. 8:1-15). They also had a close working relationship with Paul, having supported him on more than one occasion (Phil. 4:15-16; Acts 18:5; 2 Cor. 11:7-10, esp. v. 9). Paul may have visited them when Corinth was having its problems (2 Cor. 2:12-13; 7:5-6). He did keep the Passover with them in Acts 20:6. So it comes as no surprise that he would want them to have God's grace and peace. Grace is kindly acts freely given. Peace is an internal calm.

REFLECTION & DISCUSSION

1. Using the entire letter, give an explanation of Paul's circumstances at the time he wrote.

2. What does the word "saints" mean? Who would these be today?

3. Who were the bishops and what was their job?

4. What special role do deacons play?

5. Briefly describe the Philippi of Paul's day.

6. How did the first converts in Philippi become Christians?

7. Describe the Philippian church's special relationship to Paul.

8. What prayer did Paul express for them in 1:2?

2

THANKING GOD FOR PHILIPPI

PHILIPPIANS 1:3-11

THANKFUL JOY FOR PHILIPPI

Paul was beaten at Philippi and thrown in prison, yet he thanked God for the Christians there (Phil. 1:3). He always remembered them in prayer. We need to remember the power of prayer (Jas. 5:16-18). We can do nothing greater for a friend than to remember them as we approach God's throne. After all, the one who gave his life for us stands ready to mediate between us and God (1 Tim. 2:5-6). Though we may not know how or what to ask, the Holy Spirit stands ready to put our desires into words (Rom. 8:26).

Paul's prayers in behalf of the Philippian brethren were expressed with joy because of their "fellowship" with him in the gospel (Phil. 1:4-5). The word fellowship carries with it the idea of a partnership or joint participation. All Christians have an obligation to preach the gospel (Matt. 28:18-20; Mark 16:15-16). Those at Philippi partook in Paul's proclamation by praying for him and sending financial support (4:16). Such support for preaching and preachers actually began with Lydia, the first convert in the city (Acts 16:14-15). She compelled Paul's company to come into her house.

CONFIDENCE PLACED IN THE LORD

A man with a broken watch might take it to the repairman. The repairman, after examining it might say he could not fix it. The only alternative would then be to send it back to the maker. Similarly, we must turn to the Maker if we would see the church grow (Eph. 3:20-21). God, through Paul, had begun the church at Philippi. He had served as an earthen vessel to carry the precious gospel message to the lost of that city (2 Cor. 4:7).

Paul was confident God would also bring the work begun at Philippi to a good end (Phil. 2:13). He knew all in the church were a part of God's great workmanship. Every Christian's purpose was, and is, to do the good works for which he was created as a new creature (Eph. 2:10). Paul's confidence that God would finish the good work started in Philippi was based on two things. First, there was the depth of his own love for them which led him to do all he could to help them. Then, there was the partnership he had with them in the preaching of God's Word (Phil. 1:6-7).

PAUL'S PRAYER FOR THE PHILIPPIAN CHURCH

Paul prayed for the Philippians. He first called God as a witness to his love for them, which was like Christ's love (cf. 1 Cor. 11:1). He then prayed that their love might abound. This word "love" comes from the Greek word *agape* (Matt. 5:43-48). It is a love that desires the best for others (Rom. 15:2; 13:8-10; Gal. 6:10). Paul wanted that love to continue to abound. Max Hughes wrote a study guide on this book in which he suggested the word "abound" actually "signifies running over, wave upon wave."

Paul did not want their love to be misdirected, so he further prayed their love would grow in knowledge of God's will. Their knowledge needed to develop so they could understand the difference between right and wrong (Phil. 1:8-9). All Christians should grow in knowledge so that they can teach others. The Hebrew writer was concerned because those brethren had not grown into teaching. They were still like babies feeding on the milk of the word. "For everyone who partakes only of milk is unskilled in the word of righteousness, for he is a babe. But solid food belongs to those who are of full age, that is, those who by reason of use have their senses exercised to discern both good and evil" (Heb. 5:12-14).

Paul also prayed the brethren at Philippi would follow only those things that would keep them in a right relationship to God. His hope was that they would applaud, or encourage, righteous conduct (1 Thess. 5:21). He wanted them to be without any offense that might prevent them from entering heaven. Thus, he prayed they would be fruitful through Jesus (Phil. 1:10-11; Gal. 5:22-25).

REFLECTION & DISCUSSION

1. What facts make prayer a valuable tool in the Christian's life?

2. List some things about the brethren for which you are thankful.

3. How can we have lasting church growth?

4. What gave Paul confidence the work in Philippi would come to a good end?

5. What significant elements do you find in Paul's prayer for the Philippians?

6. What should we do in our prayers for the brethren?

3

PREACHING THE GOSPEL

PHILIPPIANS 1:12-18

OPPORTUNITIES FOUND IN IMPRISONMENT

Some might have thought imprisonment would have stopped Paul's work. However, Paul says God used the circumstances to present more opportunities to preach. Paul, in chains, found doors opened, which should encourage us to look for open doors in times of trouble (Phil. 1:12). Paul wrote to the Roman brethren, "And we know that all things work together for good to those who love God, to those who are the called according to His purpose" (8:28). Good can come even from the imprisonment of one of God's great preachers.

Knowledge of Paul's imprisonment was widespread and gave people cause to question as to why. Such questions gave Paul numerous chances to tell about Christ. They could bind the minister, but not his message. As he told Timothy, "Remember that Jesus Christ, of the seed of David, was raised from the dead according to my gospel, for which I suffer trouble as an evildoer, even to the point of chains; but the word of God is not chained (2 Tim. 2:8-9). Paul, in chains, was able to tell Caesar's elite that he was in bonds for Christ (Phil. 1:13).

Paul's bondage was also used by God to embolden some brethren. His willingness to die for the preaching of Jesus stood as a great example for those around him who may have formerly been fearful (Phil. 1:14). Paul's words to the Ephesian elders may very well have given them more courage to carry out God's work. He told them he did not know what would happen in Jerusalem, except that the Holy Spirit had revealed he would be put in chains and suffer through tribulations. Then, he said, "But none of these things move me; nor do I count my life dear to myself, so that I may finish my race with joy, and the ministry which I received from the Lord Jesus, to testify to the gospel of the grace of God" (Acts 20:22-24; cf. 21:13).

MOTIVES FOR PREACHING

Evidently some were jealous of Paul's success as a preacher. They promoted a party spirit by encouraging others to follow them (Phil. 1:15). Obviously, preachers who know God's purpose will seek to unite all Christians under the Lordship of Jesus with no emphasis on personal followings (1 Cor. 1:10-13). In v. 16, the word translated "selfish ambition" actually suggests they were campaigning like politicians for support. These men had the right message but he wrong motive. In 1 Cor. 16:14, Paul said, "Let all that you do be done with love." Certainly, the party spirit omitted that important element.

Others preached Christ with good will for Paul and a love for the truth. They apparently saw Paul's determination to defend the gospel and were provoked to a greater love of the truth (Phil. 1:17). We need to have the right message and the right motive. Rather than being like children who believe whatever message they last heard, we need to speak "the truth in love," so that we might "grow up in all things into Him who is the head—Christ" (Eph. 4:15). Paul's words in 1 Cor. 13:13 remind us that great works are made worthless when love is missing.

REJOICING IN THE PREACHING OF CHRIST

While some preached Christ hoping to gain a personal follow-ing, Paul was still thankful Christ was being preached (Phil. 1:18). This lets us know they were not false teachers, but preached strictly out of a wrong motive. Notice, Paul was able to rejoice even though they were politicking against him.

Remember, when Paul was blind, he waited in a house on a Straight street for someone to give him his sight and tell him what he must do. Jesus told Ananias to "Go, for he is a chosen vessel of Mine to bear My name before Gentiles, kings, and the children of Israel" (Acts 9:15). That goal dominated the rest of his life. It did not matter to him how it was accomplished. He did not worry about men get-ting the credit because he knew God was the source of any fruit that was born (1 Cor. 3:5-7).

REFLECTION & DISCUSSION

1. Use Paul's life to show how God can bring good out of bad situ-ations.

2. Why do you think prison should not be a threat to Christians?

3. What made Paul able to face trouble with such confidence?

4. What various motives might one have for preaching Christ?

5. What was the most important goal in Paul's life? What is the most important goal in your life?

4

PAUL'S EAGER LONGING

PHILIPPIANS 1:19-26

CONFIDENCE IN GOD'S POWER TO DELIVER

Even though he was in prison, Paul was confident God would deliver him (Phil. 1:19). He may have meant he was confident God would set him free from prison. However, v. 20 makes that doubtful. More likely, he is expressing his confidence that God would work it all out for good. He might be delivered from prison to preach freely again, or he might be delivered from this life and get to be with Christ.

Paul's confidence was based, in part, on the prayers of the saints in his behalf. As the apostle told the brethren in Corinth, he had to learn not to trust in himself but "in God who raises the dead, who delivered us from so great a death, and does deliver us; in whom we trust that He will still deliver us, you also helping together in prayer for us, that thanks may be given by many persons on our behalf for the gift granted to us through many" (2 Cor. 1:9-11).

His confidence also rested in the "supply" or help of the Spirit. The idea behind the word "supply" is that of a help that undergirds and strengthens. During his second imprisonment, when he had less hope of being released, Paul told Timothy, "And the Lord will deliver me from every evil work and preserve me for His heavenly kingdom. To Him be glory forever and ever. Amen" (2 Tim. 4:18)! Such thinking would surely support one through the most difficult of times.

PAUL'S EAGER LONGING

Vine says the word translated "earnest expectation" means "primarily a watching with outstretched head....signifies strained expectancy, eager longing, the stretching forth of the head indicating an expectation of something from a certain place." Paul did not look forward to failure, but to success in showing Christ more clearly to others. He might do that either through his life or death (Phil. 1:20).

He lived only to show forth the Savior. Paul could count death as gain because it would bring a long-awaited reward of rest. In fact, in one letter he wrote, "For we know that if our earthly house, this tent, is destroyed, we have a building from God, a house not made with hands, eternal in the heavens." He explained further that such knowledge made him "groan, being burdened, not because we want to be unclothed, but further clothed, that mortality may be swallowed up by life. Now He who has prepared us for this very thing is God, who also has given us the Spirit as a guarantee" (2 Cor. 5:18; 2 Tim. 4:6-8; Rev. 14:13).

One has to know how to live to be able to die with the same assurance Paul expressed (Phil. 1:21). He told the Galatian brethren, "I have been crucified with Christ; it is no longer I who live, but Christ lives in me; and the life which I now live in the flesh I live by faith in the Son of God, who loved me and gave Himself for me" (Gal. 2:20).

A DIFFICULT CHOICE

If the choice of life or death were left to him, the apostle did not know what to choose. As he saw it, continued life offered him further opportunities for service and fruit-bearing (Phil. 1:22). In fact, each day of a Christian's life should be given in service to God. Such will magnify the Lord and bring forth fruit (John 15:18).

Paul saw the choice as a difficult one. It was like going through a very narrow mountain pass. The choice was a hard one since it was between good and better. He would prefer, for his own sake, to "depart" or strike camp, and be with his Lord. The word "depart" describes a loosing of the mooring ropes or taking the harness off a weary horse at the end of the day (Phil. 1:23).

Yet there was still much good he could do for the brethren. His continued support and instruction would help them to face the adversary. So, for their sakes, the continuation of his life might have been best. He trusted God would work it out for the best. If he continued to live, Paul would work to help them develop spiritually and increase their happiness in the faith. He was certain such work to increase their faith would cause their rejoicing, or better glorying, in the Lord to increase (Phil. 1:24-26).

REFLECTION & DISCUSSION

1. What gave Paul confidence God would ultimately work to his good?

2. How could Paul consider his own death to be gain?

3. How do we need to live to die with confident assurance?

4. What type of life must Paul have lived to say, "For me to live is Christ"?

5. Read Phil. 1:24-26. What would you do if you had only a year to live?

5

A PLEA TO STAND FAST

PHILIPPIANS 1:27-30

LIVING WORTHY OF THE GOSPEL

Paul wanted the Philippian brethren to behave in a manner worthy of their citizenship in the kingdom of Christ. He told Timothy to "be an example to the believers in word, in conduct, in love, in spirit, in faith, in purity" (1 Tim. 4:12). Titus received his instructions to "speak the things which are proper for sound doctrine." Those things included the older men being "sober, reverent, temperate, sound in faith, in love, in patience." Also, sound doctrine required the older women to "be reverent in behavior, not slanderers, not given to much wine, teachers of good things." Especially they were to instruct younger Christian women in the art of loving their husbands and properly caring for their children "that the word of God may not be blasphemed" (Tit. 2:15).

He wanted their conduct to be a good example of Christian living whether he was with them or not. The Christian's life should be guided by the word and not affected by the messenger's presence or absence (John 17:17). The apostle wanted them to be united in their efforts and inner feelings about the gospel's advancement. "Now I plead with you, brethren, by the name of our Lord Jesus Christ, that you all speak the same thing, and that there be no divisions among you, but that you be perfectly joined together in the same mind and in the same judgment" (1 Cor. 1:10). Unity is a ready means of showing others the church is from God (John 17:20-21).

Paul also wanted them to stand fast like soldiers holding a firm line against the enemies' attacks. This could be done because of the assurance that our labors in accord with the Lord's will have a good reward (1 Cor. 15:58; 16:13; Eph. 6:10-18). He further asked them to fight side by side in defense of the truth. The words "striving together" describe the teamwork so necessary to win an athletic contest (Phil. 1:27).

STAND FAST WITHOUT TERROR

Paul did not want the brethren at Philippi to appear to be "terrified." Shepherd says the word "terrified carries the suggestions of the action of a horse in a race, which becomes scared and springs aside and runs off wildly." People who behaved in that fashion would be discouraged and ready to quit at the least sign of opposition. There is no doubt Christians will face opposition. Paul wrote to Timothy, "Yes, and all who desire to live godly in Christ Jesus will suffer persecution" (2 Tim. 3:12). But we need not fear because none of our enemies have the power to overthrow the kingdom or to cause us to lose our souls in eternity (Matt. 16:13-20; 10:28-31).

In contrast to a terrified existence, the firm stand Paul wanted them to take would cause their enemies to realize they were on the trail to destruction. Paul commended those at Thessalonica because their faith remained strong in the face of persecution and assured them their tormentors would be punished by God (2 Thess. 1:3-6).

Christians can face times of persecution without great fear because of the Lord's promise in the sermon on the mount (Matt. 5:10-12).

That is why the apostles rejoiced when they were counted worthy to suffer (Acts 5:41). Confident living, in place of living in terror, would also show that the Philippians had been delivered from sin (Phil. 1:28).

THE HONOR OF SUFFERING

Paul counted it an honor to be able to believe on Christ and even to suffer for him. "If we endure, we shall also reign with Him" (2 Tim. 2:12; 2 Cor. 11:23-33). Peter agreed with him when he wrote, "But even if you should suffer for righteousness' sake, you are blessed. 'And do not be afraid of their threats, nor be troubled'" (1 Pet. 3:14).

The Philippians had seen, and heard of, Paul going through times of conflict. Lipscomb believed Paul was referring to his beating and imprisonment while at Philippi (Acts 16:22-24). Certainly his reaction (Acts 16:35-40) and later reference to it (1 Thess. 2:2) indicate it was a time of agony in his mind. The Philippians were not going through anything others had not gone through. In fact, they knew Paul was again suffering for the truth in Roman imprisonment (Phil. 1:29-30).

REFLECTION & DISCUSSION

1. What type of life did Paul urge Timothy, Titus, and the Philippians to live?

2. Give some examples of the good that can come out of such a life.

3. Why does the Christian not have to live in terror?

4. What effect should our confident living have on those who oppose us?

5. Describe some of the suffering endured by New Testament Christians. Why should we be honored to suffer for Christ?

6

THE HUMBLE MIND

PHILIPPIANS 2:1-11

BLESSINGS SURELY BELONGING TO CHRISTIANS

The "ifs" of Phil. 2:1 were not meant to question, but to be a plain statement of fact. The word "since" might better suggest the meaning to modern readers. Paul is listing things which should cause Christians to be united. First, there is a consolation in Christ. Literally, Vine says the word means "a calling to one's side". Christ calls us to come to his side by doing his will. We are thereby released from our burden of sin. We can look forward to entering the kingdom of heaven at his side as well (Matt. 11:28-30; 7:21-23). Also, Christ is at our side to plead our case, which is the meaning of the word "advocate" in 1 John 2:1.

Second, God has comforted us lovingly in our time of affliction. Paul described God as the "God of all comfort, who comforts us in all our tribulation, that we may be able to comfort those who are in any trouble, with the comfort with which we ourselves are comforted of God" (2 Cor. 3:3-7). Third, we have the fellowship of the Holy Spirit. The idea is that we are in partnership with the Spirit (Acts 5:32). Our mind becomes like His through reading the word.

Fourth, there is the tender mercy and compassion God has for us. The King James Version has "if any bowels and mercies." The Greek word for bowels was their expression for the seat of the emotions, which would be comparable to our word "heart." Certainly, God gave man the one gift that touched the deepest part of his emotions. Jesus told Nicodemus, "For God so loved the world that He gave His only begotten Son, that whoever believes in Him should not perish but have everlasting life" (John 3:16). Because God had such mercy and compassion, we ought to have the same for our fellow Christians.

COMPLETING PAUL'S JOY THROUGH UNITY

The Philippian church had already given Paul much cause for rejoicing (1:4; 4:1). He pleaded with them to complete his joy by being united in thought, love, work, and purpose. Even elders are not to be self-willed (Tit. 1:7). Christians agree in biblical principle. That agreement can form the basis of a working relationship that would produce a likemindedness (Phil. 2:2).

To avoid division, they would have to avoid selfish ambition, or the promotion of a party spirit for personal gain (1:16; 3 John 9-11). Conceit is very similar to selfish ambition. It is a desire to have self lifted into a high, honored position in men's eyes. In place of these things, we should be humble, which is another way of saying lowliness of mind (1 Pet. 5:6). We should learn to appreciate, even look for, the good qualities of others. We should always treat the other man as one who is worthy of our service (Phil. 2:3).

Consideration for others' needs, in the Christian life, must come before self. As Paul told the Roman brethren, "Be kindly affectionate to one another with brotherly love, in honor giving preference to one another" (Rom. 12:10; John 13:34-35; 1 John 3:10-11, 18). Of course, this is not the interest shown by a busybody, but the genuine concern of one who would help another bear his burdens (Phil. 2:4; Gal. 6:2).

THE MIND OF CHRIST

In continuing the ideas of unity and the consideration of others which promotes it, Paul refers to Christ. He wanted the Philippians to have the same disposition, or attitude as Christ. To live like Christ, one must think like Christ thought and live accordingly (1 Pet. 2:21). Before Christ came to earth, he existed as the very essence of God. We might say it was his nature to be God. "He is the image of the invisible God, the firstborn over all creation" (Col. 1:15; Heb. 1:3; John 5:17-18; 1:13). When Paul describes our Lord as the firstborn, in this passage, he means the preeminent one. Jesus did not exploit, or hold on to at all cost, his equality with God, but was willing to give it up for the sake of man and in obedience to God (Phil. 2:5-6).

To do that, he had to give up the power, glory, and worship that belonged to him as God. The American Standard Version says he "emptied" himself. The idea is that he sacrificed his glory and took the nature of man. John told the early church, "In the beginning was the Word, and the Word was with God, and the Word was God. ... And the Word became flesh and dwelt among us, and we beheld His glory, the glory as of the only begotten of the Father, full of grace and truth" (John 1:1, 14; 17:5; 2 Cor. 8:9). To come to earth as a man, Christ truly had to empty himself of all the splendor of the Godhead.

There are two senses in which Christ took the form of a servant. First, man was created as a servant. His whole existence is fulfilled in obedient service to God (Eccl. 12:13). When Jesus took man's likeness, he took the form of a servant. Second, he came to serve man, not be served (John 13:1-17; Luke 22:24-27; Mark 9:35; 10:43-45). As God, he did not have to die, but he chose to lay down his life for our sakes (Phil. 2:78; John 10:17-18; Heb. 2:14-15). He did it because of the joy that would result from his sacrifice, despite having to suffer the worst death known (Heb. 12:2; Deut. 21:22-23; Gal. 3:13). To come to earth, Jesus gave up the form that naturally accrues to being God and took the figure of a man (John 4:24; Luke 24:39). Jesus is now glorified man, which we hope to be one day (1 John 3:2).

GOD HAS EXALTED CHRIST

Jesus prayed just before his death that God would glorify him again as he had been glorified before the world was (John 17:5). Because Jesus lowered himself to lift man up, God exalted him more than ever before (Rom. 1:34; Matt. 28:18). Remember, Jesus taught that the man who humbled himself would be exalted (Matt. 23:12; Luke 14:11; 18:14). The "name" God gave Jesus would appear to be that of Lord. Man had lowered, or humiliated, Christ as much as he could, but God raised him up to be master of all who would be saved (Phil. 2:9; John 14:6; Acts 2:32-36; Eph. 1:22-23; 1 Tim. 2:5).

Isaiah 45:23 says every knee will bow to God. Clearly, then, Paul is ascribing deity to Jesus when he says every knee will bow at the sound of his name (Phil. 2:10-11). We can recognize Jesus now and submit to him, (Rom. 10:9-10; Matt. 10:32-33), thereby becoming one God will confess in heaven. Or we can wait and acknowledge him as the conquering Lord who has come to reclaim his own. Thus, we would make ourselves one of his enemies who will be made subject to him at the time of his second coming (1 Cor. 15:24-26). The choice of the time when we will confess his Lordship is left up to us. In either event, we should remember when man confesses Jesus as Lord, God is glorified (John 17:1).

REFLECTION & DISCUSSION

1. Name four things Paul says surely belong to Christians.

2. Why do you think Paul saw the unity of the Philippians as a means of completing his joy?

3. What is strife? What actions might lead to strife in the church?

4. What is the mind of Christ? What could you do to exhibit such?

5. When and how is Christ glorified?

7

LETTING THE LIGHT SHINE

PHILIPPIANS 2:12-18

THE IMPORTANCE OF OBEDIENCE

As we saw in the last lesson, Christ's life stands as the greatest example of obedience. Because of Christ's example, Paul challenged the Philippian Christians to obey. The writer of Hebrews said, "Though He was a Son, yet He learned obedience by the things which He suffered. And having been perfected, He became the author of eternal salvation to all who obey Him" (Heb. 5:8-9). Paul urged the brethren to have such obedience as a constant goal in their lives.

Christ is going to punish those who do not keep on obeying the gospel (2 Thess. 1:7-9). Those in the church at Philippi had started well on the road of obedience with Paul present. In this letter, he expresses a desire for them to continue even in his absence. "Work out" carries with it the thought of working to full completion. It is like working out a math problem. In other words, do not stop until you have attained the final goal of salvation. It is evident the inspired apostle believed in individual accountability.

In fact, Paul wrote of his concern for his own salvation. "But I discipline my body and bring it into subjection, lest, when I have preached to others, I myself should become disqualified" (1 Cor. 9:27). Similarly, the Hebrew brethren were warned to be aware of the danger of drifting (Heb. 2:14). No wonder Paul told those at Philippi they ought to hold God in awe and tremble at the possibility of failing to do his will (Phil. 2:12; Isa. 66:2). "Therefore let him who thinks he stands take heed lest he fall" (1 Cor. 10:12).

GOD WORKS IN CHRISTIANS

When Christians submit their lives to God's will, it can be said that God works in them (Phil. 2:13). The Almighty works in them through his great plan for man's salvation. "But we are bound to give thanks to God always for you, brethren beloved by the Lord, because God from the beginning chose you for salvation through sanctification by the Spirit and belief in the truth" (2 Thess. 2:13). God also works in Christians as they live for Christ each day. Paul said, "I have been crucified with Christ; it is no longer I who live, but Christ lives in me; and the life which I now live in the flesh I live by faith in the Son of God, who loved me and gave Himself for me" (Gal. 2:20).

The follower of Christ needs to carry out his works for God without complaint or question. To do otherwise is to risk giving others grounds for just criticism. Also, God is not pleased with those who murmur. "Nor murmur, as some of them also murmured, and were destroyed by the destroyer" (1 Cor. 10:10).

Christians must have a pure character. If their actions involve no wrong, and their motives are free from wrong, the name of the church will not be hurt because of them. This will also help Christ's followers to be more like God in nature every day. They will stand out as examples of good in the middle of wicked people. The truth will thus be held forth for the world to see. Paul told the brethren that living in the way just described would mean his labors in Philippi would come to a fruitful end at the judgment. Christians can only be the light of the world when they hold up the word of truth (Phil. 2:14-16). Remember, Jesus said, "Let your light so shine before men, that they may see your good works and glorify your Father in heaven" (Matt. 5:16).

PAUL'S WILLINGNESS TO SACRIFICE

Paul had so absorbed Christ's qualities that he was ready to die that the greater sacrifice of their lives of faith might be enhanced. He saw his death as a drink offering poured out on the altar. Often, drink offerings preceded other sacrifices to God. Paul rejoiced over any opportunity to serve. He knew they would likewise rejoice in opportunities to serve as he served, thus joining him in sacrificial service to God (Phil. 2:17-18).

REFLECTION & DISCUSSION

1.   What means should you use to "work out your own salvation?"

2.   Name some ways God works in us as Christians.

3. What complaints and forms of questioning should we avoid?

4. What could you do this week to let your light shine to God's glory?

5. For what ultimate purpose was Paul willing to sacrifice himself?

8

TWO FAITHFUL SERVANTS

PHILIPPIANS 2:19-30

TIMOTHY

Paul was able to broaden his service to the various churches by sending faithful messengers to them. He hoped it would be the Lord's will that Timothy could soon be sent to check on the welfare of the church at Philippi. When he had delivered word from Paul to them, he could report back to the apostle the things he had seen in the church. It is obvious Paul expected the report to be good, as he said it would comfort him (Phil. 2:19).

Of those available to him, Timothy was the one Paul could depend upon to be concerned only for the welfare of the church (Phil. 2:20). He told the Corinthian brethren, "Now if Timothy comes, see that he may be with you without fear; for he does the work of the Lord, as I also do" (1 Cor. 16:10). Paul's confidence in this young preacher can be seen in the descriptive words he uses in several letters. He called him a fellow worker, "true son in the faith," and a brother who had preached among the Corinthians (Rom. 16:21; 1 Tim. 1:2, 18; 2 Tim. 1:2; 2 Cor. 1:1, 19).

When Paul's concern for the church at Thessalonica could no longer be contained, he said, "We thought it good to be left in Athens alone, and sent Timothy, our brother and minister of God, and our fellow laborer in the gospel of Christ, to establish you and encourage you concerning your faith" (1 Thess. 3:12).

Others sought only their own personal gain. But Timothy, like a coin or precious metal that had been proven genuine, was known as one who loved the church as dearly as Paul, his father in the faith. As soon as Paul knew how his trial would go, Timothy would be sent. Perhaps all other helpers had been sent on missions by Paul. Paul believed in God's providence and felt sure he would soon be released so he could visit Philippi firsthand (Phil. 2:21-24).

EPAPHRODITUS

It is possible Epaphroditus was the one who carried this letter to the Philippians. "Your messenger" could be translated "your epistle" if he was the one sent. He was a brother in Christ, a coworker in furthering the gospel, and one who had fought side by side with Paul in defense of the gospel. He was their apostle, messenger, sent on a mission to Paul. Evidently, he was the one sent with provision for Paul's needs (4:10, 18). He likewise stayed with Paul to attend to further needs that might have arisen (Phil. 2:25).

It appears Epaphroditus' physical sickness made him homesick. His longing for home was intensified because he heard that they had learned of his illness. Paul said he nearly died. He thanked God for his recovery. Why did Paul not miraculously heal him? Coffman reminds us of "the purpose of miracles which were never given for the personal needs of God's apostles and preachers, but only for the purpose of 'confirming the word'" (Phil. 2:26-27; Mark 16:20). The writer of Hebrews asked, "How shall we escape if we neglect so great a salvation, which at the first began to be spoken by the Lord, and was confirmed to us by those who heard Him, God also bearing witness both with signs and wonders, with various miracles, and gifs of the Holy Spirit, according to His own will?" (Heb. 2:3-4).

When Epaphroditus had recovered, Paul sent him home. Paul knew such an action would bring joy to those at Philippi, Epaphroditus, and himself. Paul could have been selfish and kept him for personal service, but got more joy out of knowing the brethren's minds were eased. The apostle directed the church to receive their messenger back with gladness and to hold him in esteem. After all, he had risked his life in Christ's service on their behalf (Phil. 2:28-30).

REFLECTION & DISCUSSION

1. Describe some of the uses Paul found for other faithful messengers.

2. How did Paul regard Timothy? List words and verses supporting your answer.

3. In what ways did Paul use Timothy?

4. Why did Epaphroditus go to Paul? What happened while he was there?

5. Why did Paul send him home? How did he expect him to be received?

9

THE VALUE OF KNOWING CHRIST

PHILIPPIANS 3:1-11

BEWARE OF DOGS

The word "finally," according to Vine, was sometimes used by Paul to mark the close of one part of an epistle. It is a transitional word that actually means, "And for the rest." Paul wanted the brethren to rejoice in the Lord, but *only* in the Lord. The "same things" he wrote about may be the rejoicing just mentioned, or, the message that follows about those who would require Gentiles to be circumcised. The latter seems most likely since he had just been to the Jerusalem conference before his first visit to Philippi (Acts 15:1-29). Paul did not mind repetition. In fact, repetition aids learning, as any good teacher knows, and it was needful for the safety of their souls (Phil. 3:1).

It was common for Jews to deride Gentiles by calling them dogs. Max Hughes points out that during those days dogs were dirty animals that roamed the streets eating garbage. They were half-wild and dangerous (Psa. 22:1620). These the apostle spoke of worked, but to an evil end (Matt. 23:15; 2 Cor. 11:12-15; Gal. 1:6-9). It appears Paul is referring to the Judaizers who were trying to make Gentile

Christians obey the law of Moses (Acts 15:5; Gal. 3:24-25). They asked Gentiles to circumcise to be more pleasing to God, but it did not please God, so it was only a mutilation of the flesh, or concision (Phil. 3:2; Lev. 21:5).

The Jews used their fleshly circumcision to prove they were descendants of the faithful Abraham. However, Christians were the ones truly circumcised in accord with God's will. When one is baptized into Christ, he has the sins of the flesh cut away and begins to walk as a spiritual servant of God (Col. 2:10-13; Gal. 6:11-16). God wants inward commitment more than outward ritual (Rom. 2:25-29). Now, God's true Israel is composed of those who worship him in spirit (John 4:23-24; Matt. 15:7-9). The Christian's glory is not in the flesh or outward works, but in Christ (Gal. 6:14). God never intended to accept mere outward ritual (cf. Lev. 26; esp. vv. 31, 40-42; Deut. 10:15-16; 30:5-6; Jer. 4:4; Ezek. 44:6-8). The one who trusts in the flesh tries to pull himself up by his own bootstraps, thus rejecting Christ's assistance (Phil. 3:3).

PAUL'S FLESHLY ACCOMPLISHMENTS

Paul was not putting down Judaism because he had a low place in it. Here was a man who truly could have, if anyone could, placed confidence in fleshly accomplishments. Paul's list of credentials shows he was a Jew in high standing. Lipscomb tells us the Ishmaelite was circumcised at the age of 13 and the proselyte in mature life when he accepted Judaism. The apostle to the Gentiles was born a Jew and circumcised on the eighth day, in accord with the Law. He was born an Israelite, one of God's people.

Paul says he was of the tribe of Benjamin. Wiersbe reminds us that Benjamin and Joseph were Jacob's favorites. Saul, the king, came from Benjamin and that tribe remained loyal during the rebellion of

Absalom. The apostle was also a Hebrew born of Hebrew parents. He was a Pharisee, which was a sect that set up strict rules to live by (Acts 23:6-9; 7:54-8:3; 9:12). His reputation for trying to keep every detail of this legalistic, outer righteousness was blameless (Phil. 3:4-6; Gal. 1:13-14).

PAUL GAVE UP ALL FOR CHRIST

Because of the above list, Paul had once counted himself a spiritual millionaire. At the time he wrote this letter, he saw himself as bankrupt before he found Christ (Matt. 5:3; Mark 8:34-38; Eph. 2:8-9; Tit. 3:5). To become a Christian, Paul had set aside the pride of the self-made man (Phil. 3:7).

Paul forfeited, or suffered the loss, of all he once held dear and counted it a good swap for the knowledge of Christ (Matt. 13:44-46). Jesus says we can either deny/forfeit self or be cast away (Luke 9:23-25; the words "cast away" and "suffered the loss" come from the same Greek word). Shepherd says "knowledge" is much more than intellectual. It "includes faith, service, sacrifice, and is analogous to the phrase 'to be in Christ' the spiritual knowledge by which the individual becomes one with Christ, so that his whole life is lived in Christ and he has no consciousness of being apart from Christ." This kind of knowledge would, of course, grow as one grew in service of the master. Paul said he counted all that was once important to him as refuse to win Christ (Phil. 3:8).

To be found in Christ, one must be baptized into him (Rom. 6:3-4). Once Paul was in Christ, he ceased relying on personal accomplishments to save him. Instead, he was obedient, which is generally the meaning of faith in the New Testament (Rom. 1:5; 16:26). As Coffman says, "The contrast is between trusting in the ceremonies of the Law of Moses for salvation as contrasted with believing and obeying the gospel of Christ."

The only faith that God will count for righteousness is that which comes by an obedient hearing of God's word (Rom. 10:17). The "faith of Christ" would refer to the Savior's faithfulness, or fidelity, in carrying out God's plan for saving man. Note that he had to obey God to be truly faithful in carrying out God's will (Phil. 2:8; John 4:24; 6:38; Matt. 26:39). Our righteousness comes by Christ's faith in that we are cleansed by his blood (Phil. 3:9; Eph. 1:7).

THE ULTIMATE GOAL: KNOWING CHRIST

The apostle's ultimate goal was knowing Christ. "Know" in Scripture usually suggests an intimate relation with someone (cf. Gen. 4:1). The Christian's purpose is to know Christ, not merely facts about him. Christ's resurrection proved he was the Son of God (Rom. 1:4). It is the basis of the Christian's appeal to obey him (Acts 2:22-36; 13:30-39). The only way anyone can know the power of his resurrection is by being buried with him and raised to walk a new life (Rom. 6:31; 8:10-13). The Christian's salvation and hope depend on Christ's resurrection (1 Cor. 15:17). His followers have fellowship, which is to share or have in common, Christ's suffering (1 Pet. 4:13; 2 Cor. 1:5-7; 2 Tim. 2:12). Sharing with Christ in suffering for righteousness will help one to be constantly dead to sin, as Christ died for sin (Phil. 3:10; Gal. 2:20).

Paul recognized the danger of failing to remain faithful (Heb. 3:14; 1 Cor. 9:27), so he used the word "if." He knew all would be raised (2 Cor. 5:10; John 5:28-29). His goal of attaining the resurrection must refer to his longing for the resurrection of the righteous to go be with the Lord (Phil. 3:11; 1 Thess. 4:13-18).

REFLECTION & DISCUSSION

1. Who do you think Paul called dogs? Why?

2. Describe the circumcision in which Christians must participate.

3. List Paul's fleshly accomplishments.

4. Why was Paul willing to give all of those up.

5. What is involved in truly knowing Christ?

10

PRESSING TOWARD THE HEAVENLY GOAL

PHILIPPIANS 3:12-16

PAUL DID NOT COUNT HIMSELF AS SUCCESSFUL

Despite all the good he had done, Paul could still say he needed to grow in the Lord's service. It will be remembered, from the last lesson, that Paul hoped to attain unto the resurrection from the dead and heaven. The Lord chose Paul to bear the good news of salvation to the Gentiles (Acts 9:15). Paul wanted to gain the salvation he had spoken to others about. Though he was an apostle and had labored hard for the Lord, he did not count himself as having reached the heavenly goal. Certainly we could say this verse suggests the possibility of apostasy (Phil. 3:12).

The only time Paul was willing to say he had run the race completely and would receive the crown was when he was about to die. He told Timothy, "For I am already being poured out as a drink offering, and the time of my departure is at hand. I have fought the good fight, I have finished the race, I have kept the faith. Finally, there is laid up for me the crown of righteousness, which the Lord, the righteous Judge, will give to me on that Day" (2 Tim. 4:6-8).

FORGETTING THE PAST

Before he faced death, Paul always had a singleminded purpose. To achieve his purpose, Paul put the past out of his mind. Wiersbe says to forget in the Bible means "no longer to be influenced by or affected by." Christians need to forget past sins, accomplishments, and wrongs suffered at the hands of others.

The first thing anyone needs to forget from their past is the sins they have committed. On Pentecost following Christ's resurrection from the dead, Peter told the assembled multitude God had verified Jesus' Sonship through the miracles he worked. Yet, they, with lawless hands, took him and killed him. Peter proclaimed, "Therefore let all the house of Israel know assuredly that God has made this Jesus, whom you crucified, both Lord and Christ." Realizing their sinfulness, they asked, "Men and brethren, what shall we do?" Peter said, "Repent, and let every one of you be baptized in the name of Jesus Christ for the remission of sins; and you shall receive the gift of the Holy Spirit." Those who have repented of their sins and been baptized in the name of Jesus can forget whatever sins they committed in the past because God has blotted out their sins (Acts 2:22-23, 36-38; 3:19).

Sometimes one will be held back by good things in his past. He may dwell on past achievements and fail to continue doing good. The church at Ephesus got off to a good start, but they could not rely on those good deeds they had done to keep them pleasing in the Lord's sight. The Lord had to warn them, by saying, "Nevertheless I have this against you, that you have left your first love. Remember from where you have fallen; repent and do the first works, or else I will come to you quickly and remove your lampstand from its place unless you repent" (Rev. 2:4-5). Clearly, past accomplishments must be forgotten, and good works continued.

Many are held back from doing good because of some wrong

they have suffered at someone else's hands. Their whole life is wrapped up in getting even. Joseph is one of the best examples of one who was able to forget wrongs others had committed against him. He told his brothers God had used their mistreatment of him to achieve a good end (Gen. 50:20). God can still take the good and the bad in our lives and make it work together for our good (Phil. 3:13; Rom. 8:28).

PRESSING ON TO THE PRIZE

Having forgotten all that was in the past, the apostle pressed, or stretched forward like a runner trying to break the tape, toward the prize of salvation in Christ (Phil. 3:14; Eph. 1:18; Heb. 3:1). The writer of Hebrews used the image of a race to help his readers see the importance of setting aside those things that might hinder them on their way to heaven. "Therefore we also, since we are surrounded by so great a cloud of witnesses, let us lay aside every weight, and the sin which so easily ensnares us, and let us run with endurance the race that is set before us" (Heb. 12:1). To reach the goal, each follower of Christ should focus on the Lord who has already endured hardship and is now seated at God's right hand (12:12, 12-14).

While Paul still had room for growth (v. 12), he was mature or full grown. He asked all those who were also mature to keep their minds set on the goal. It is not time to sit down when the race is still ongoing. If they would continue in a singleminded pursuit of God's reward, Paul assured them that God would reveal to them any imperfection they still had. Meanwhile, he urged them to continue in that which they knew to be right (Phil. 3:15-16).

REFLECTION & DISCUSSION

1. How does a Christian measure true success?

2. How can someone cease to be influenced by past sins?

3. What dangers do you see in seeking revenge?

4. In what sense can dwelling on past accomplishments be a bad thing?

5. What is the ultimate goal of all who follow Christ?

11

CITIZENSHIP IN HEAVEN

PHILIPPIANS 3:17-21

BE CAREFUL WHO YOU FOLLOW

Paul wanted the brethren at Philippi to follow him in his constant run toward the goal and mark. He also encouraged them to note those who followed a similar course (Phil. 3:17; 1 Cor. 11:1). The writer of Hebrews instructed his readers to "Remember those who rule over you, who have spoken the word of God to you, whose faith follow, considering the outcome of their conduct" (13:7).

The apostle also warned them against some who claimed to be Christians, yet were enemies of the cross. A warning about false teachers is a recurrent theme in Paul's preaching. He urged the elders from Ephesus to watch out for themselves and the flock they had been appointed to oversee. "For I know this, that after my departure savage wolves will come in among you, not sparing the flock. Also from among yourselves men will rise up, speaking perverse things, to draw away the disciples after themselves." He instructed them to keep a careful watch, while remembering the way he had warned them constantly with tears for three years. He told them their best defense was God's

Word. After all, it was able to give them strength and prepare them for a heavenly home (Acts 20:28-32; Rom. 16:17; 2 Thess. 3:6, 14).

One should not be misled into thinking Paul hated the false teachers. He cried over the state they were in, but warned brethren not to follow them. Their god was service to selfish interest. They were proud of things of which they should have been ashamed. Their minds were set on earthly things (Phil. 3:18-19; Col. 3:1-12).

CITIZENS OF HEAVEN

The Philippian brethren would have understood very well what the apostle meant when he said a Christian's citizenship is in heaven. Remember that many of the people at Philippi were Roman citizens. A baby born at Philippi should have had its name recorded in Rome. They would have enjoyed the rewards of Roman citizenship, though away from Rome.

Wiersbe states, "The spiritually minded believer is not attracted by the 'things' of this world. He makes his decisions on the basis of eternal values and not the passing fads of society." Lot chose the fertile plain of Jordan because of its productive value. He did not take time to consider the moral decay that finally cost him everything (Gen. 13:5-13; 18:16-19:28). Abraham, on the other hand, let God be his guide because his mind was set on heaven (Heb. 11:8-10).

In similar fashion, the Christian should long for heaven and live as if it was his goal (2 Cor. 5:110). Paul concludes the verse by saying that Christians look forward to Christ's second coming. If more emphasis were placed upon the Lord's return, greater commitment and joy would be ours (Phil. 3:20; Matt. 25:1-13; 1 Thess. 4:13-18).

The Lord will, at his coming, change this mortal body into an immortal one fitted for heaven (Phil. 3:21; 1 Cor. 15:42-53; 1 John 3:2). Instead of "lowly body" as we find here, it would be better to put "the body of our humiliation," as the American Standard Version does. The body is not despised by God. However, it is in our physical body that sin has been committed, and the terrible reward of death was faced (Rom. 7:23-24). Paul assures us that the same power Christ has to cause his enemies to submit to his will enables him to effect a great change in our bodies.

REFLECTION & DISCUSSION

1. Who should a Christian follow? What conditions should be met?

2. What types of things did Paul observe about the false teachers?

3. Explain Roman citizenship, especially as it applied to Philippi.

4. What impact should heavenly citizenship have on the Christian?

5. Explain how the Lord's coming relates to the Christian's body.

12

FOLLOWING THE GOD OF PEACE

PHILIPPIANS 4:1-9

STAND FAST IN THE LORD

In Phil. 3, Paul warned of the danger of false teachers. He stressed the importance of having heaven as one's only goal. He also pointed toward heaven as the place where Christ's followers maintain their citizenship. Because of all these things, the apostle went on to encourage the brethren to "stand fast," like soldiers holding position in the thick of battle.

As he was urging them to stand fast, Paul used four different expressions to show his deep feelings for the Christians at Philippi. They were his "beloved," which Thayer says was a tender address used for one who was esteemed, dear, or a favorite. Naturally, with those types of feelings accompanied by a long period of separation, Paul could also say he longed for them. As Thayer says, they were a cause of joy even in the apostle's imprisonment. Further, he viewed them as being like a victor's crown or a crown given to honor a guest at a banquet (Phil. 4:1).

DIRECTIONS TO TWO CHRISTIAN WOMEN

Paul beseeched two women by name. He did not take sides, but asked each to change. He wanted them to lay aside their differences and be united in purpose in the Lord's service. Paul asked an unnamed coworker to help these women lay aside their differences. The women had been great helpers in the service to the Lord. They had helped Paul, Clement and others, "whose names are in the Book of life." It is wonderful to realize God keeps an active list of those who will inherit eternal life. Anyone can be on it if he will only be a faithful servant (Phil. 4:2-3; Acts 2:47; 1 Cor. 9:27).

Jesus told his disciples to "rejoice because your names are in heaven" (Luke 10:20). The writer of Hebrews addressed his readers as "the general assembly and church of the firstborn who are registered in heaven" (12:23). Similarly, the Lord promised, "He who overcomes shall be clothed in white garments, and I will not blot out his name from the Gook of Life; but I will confess his name before My Father and before His angels" (Rev. 3:5).

MAINTAINING THE RIGHT FRAME OF MIND

Paul was in a Roman prison, yet he could tell those in the Philippian church, "Rejoice...rejoice". The reason for this can only be that he was "in the Lord" and knew all would work out for his good (Rom. 8:28-29; 2 Tim. 1:12). He knew his labor would not come to naught (Phil. 4:4; 1 Cor. 15:58).

Along with rejoicing, Paul taught them to have a gentle demeanor that does not insist on its own rights. Hughes suggests the father in the story of the prodigal son as a good example of this (Luke 15:11-32). This should especially be done since, "The Lord is at hand." The Christian has strength to forbear because the Lord is always close to help us (Matt. 28:20; Psa. 145:18-19.) It might also be said that the Lord's return should always be counted as near, since we do not know when he will come and must be prepared (Phil. 4:5; Matt. 25:1-13).

In using the word "anxious," which Wiersbe says literally means "to be pulled in different directions," Paul is saying the Christian should not let even one thing cause him to fear so as to be pulled away from his hope (Heb. 2:1; 3:12-13; Matt. 6:25-34). It is alright to take care of the physical (1 Tim. 5:8; 2 Thess. 3:6-15), but not to the point of neglecting the spiritual. Instead, Christians should approach God and ask his help in times of need. Of course, those who remember to tell him their needs should be sure to remember to thank him (Eph. 5:20; Luke 17:11-19). If Christ's followers would take "everything" to God in prayer, including the little things, they might not have so many big things to take to him (Phil. 4:6).

The result of taking all to God in prayer will be an inner tranquility given by God to the believer (John 14:27). This peace will stand like a military guard over the minds of those in Christ Jesus. No one looking at this peace from a human standpoint can understand it. Neither can the one who possesses such peace fully understand or explain it, but they would not give it up (Phil. 4:7; Isa, 26:3).

THINKING ON THINGS THAT WILL YIELD THE PEACE OF GOD

Those things given thoughtful consideration will have a great impact on one's life (Prov. 23;7; 4:23; Matt. 12:34). Knowing this, Paul gave a list of things to think on. He would have Christians think on "true things," which would be things in accord with God's word (John 17:17). "Noble things" would be reverend, serious, combining a sense or gravity and dignity. The word "just" indicates right conduct. "Pure" is used only for those things not contaminated. Pleasing and agreeable things would be "lovely." Only those things with a good reputation would qualify as being "of good report."

The *New Bible Commentary: Revised* suggests that "virtue" is moral excellence. Paul wanted the church at Philippi to love so as to show a moral excellence and praiseworthy type of conduct. To do that, he told them they would have to give close attention to those things just mentioned (Phil. 4:8).

Paul had both taught them and shown them how to live the Christian life. So, he urged them to go on from right thought to right action (1 Cor. 11:1). Such would result in God, who is the source of peace, being with them (Phil. 4:9; cf. v. 7).

REFLECTION & DISCUSSION

1. What four expressions of tender feelings did Paul use for the brethren in Philippi? What do you suppose could cause him to feel the way he did?

2. How could his directions to two women help solve our problems today?

3. Where is true cause for rejoicing found? Why?

4. What things can a Christian do to have peace instead of anxiety?

5. What special things should Christians think on? Why?

13

FELLOWSHIP IN PREACHING

PHILIPPIANS 4:10-23

THE LORD ENABLED PAUL IN ALL CIRCUMSTANCES

The church in Philippi had sent Paul a gift just before he wrote this letter. Their help was not something new, but a revival of a good work they had done before. From what the apostle also says, it seems they had wanted to help but had been hindered in some way. Max Hughes says "their lack was not sympathy but of opportunity" (Phil. 4:10).

Even today, as this passage is read, it might appear Paul was suffering through some time of great deprivation. However, Paul said such was not the case because he had learned to be content, or live without assistance, no matter what physical circumstances were his. Notice, he had to learn. It did not come naturally. Paul knew how to suffer through sparse times (2 Cor. 11:7) and times of plenty. His joy was not based upon his economic status of the moment (Phil. 4:11-12).

Paul could be content no matter what his circumstances because he was in Christ (cf. Eph. 1:3-4, 6-7, 10-11; 2:4-6, 13). Instead of "through Christ," the American Standard Version has "in him," which reminds us of the location of Paul's rejoicing as was seen in v. 4. Any true follower of Christ can be confident that all will work out for his good in Christ (Phil. 4:13; 2 Cor. 2:14a; Rom. 8:28, 35-39).

THANKFULNESS FOR A GENEROUS CHURCH

Paul did not want to seem ungrateful, so he commended the Philippian church for their good work. They shared, or had part in, his suffering when they helped. Actually, our word, "fellowship" would fit here in place of the word "shared" (Phil. 4:14).

From Paul's very first experience with the church at Philippi, he had found them to be generous, always ready to supply his needs. Paul went from Philippi to Thessalonica, then Athens and Corinth (Acts 17:1, 15-16; 18:1). We know Paul received help while in Corinth (2 Cor. 11:9). This probably came from Philippi, since we know Thessalonica had no part in it (1 Thess. 2:9; 2 Thess. 3:8). In fact, they sent for him while he was in Thessalonica, another Macedonia town (Phil. 4:15-16).

BLESSINGS ARE FOUND IN GIVING

Paul was not concerned about material provision for himself, but was glad because they would be blessed for it (Phil. 4:17). The apostle told the Ephesian elders "I have shown you in every way, by laboring like this, that you must support the weak. And remember the words of the Lord Jesus, that He said, 'It is more blessed to give than to receive'" (Acts 20:35).

Their gift had completely taken care of his needs and went up before God as a pleasing sacrifice (Phil. 4:18). The wording here reminds us of God's response to Noah's sacrifice when he got off the ark, as well as God's instructions in the Law of Moses and his words to Israel through Ezekiel (Gen. 8:20-22; Exod. 29:18; Ezek. 20:40-41).

As a result of their providing for Paul's needs, Paul told them God would provide for their needs (2 Cor. 9:6-10). Notice, it is needs, not wants, for which God will make provision (Matt. 6:24-34; 2 Cor. 12:7-9.) He will pour out to us from his riches. Once again, Paul reminded them the provision would be through Christ (Phil. 4:19).

CLOSING WORDS

Paul reminded the Philippian brethren that all praise and glory rightly belong to God. In the sermon on the mount, Christ told his disciples, "Let your light so shine before men, that they may see your good works and glorify your Father in heaven" (Matt. 5:16). The apostle, knowing the truthfulness of his statement, adds the word "Amen," which Shepherd says means, "so it is," or "so it shall be" (Phil. 4:20; Neh. 8:6; Psa. 41:13; 1 Cor. 14:15-16).

Paul wanted to say hello to all, overlooking none. He loved all of them and expressed that love with prayers for only the best in their lives. Those with Paul, the Roman brethren and even some in Caesar's service, also wished them well and sent greetings. Paul concluded, as he started, with a prayer that grace continue with all of them. Grace is, after all, our only means of salvation (Phil. 4:21-23).

REFLECTION & DISCUSSION

1. What had been lacking in the Philippian brethren's care for Paul?

2. Did contentment come naturally for Paul? Explain how such may have occurred.

3. What two types of times had Paul lived through? How was he able to do so?

4. What attitude had Paul found in the church in Philippi? In what did they share, or have fellowship with Paul?

5. What benefits resulted from their gift to Paul? Who received those benefits? How, or from whom?

6. What lessons can we learn today from Paul's closing words?

PERSONAL NOTES

PERSONAL NOTES

PERSONAL NOTES

PERSONAL NOTES

PERSONAL NOTES

PERSONAL NOTES

PERSONAL NOTES

PERSONAL NOTES

PERSONAL NOTES

PERSONAL NOTES

PERSONAL NOTES

PERSONAL NOTES

PERSONAL NOTES

BIBLIOGRAPHY

Coffman, James Burton. *Commentary on Galatians Ephesians Philippians Colossians*. Austin: Firm Foundation Publishing House, 1977.

Harrell, Pat Edwin. *The Letter of Paul to The Philippians*. Austin: R. B. Sweet Co., Inc., 1969.

Hiebert, D. Edmond. *An Introduction to the Pauline Epistles*. Chicago: Moody Press, 1971.

Lipscomb, David. *A Commentary on the New Testament Epistles*. Volume IV. Nashville: Gospel Advocate Company, 1939.

Robertson, A. T. *Paul's Joy in Christ: Studies in Philippians*. Nashville: Broadman Press, 1979.

Thayer, Joseph Henry. *A GreekEnglish Lexicon of the New Testament*. Grand Rapids: Baker Book House, 1977.

Wiersbe, Warren W. *Be Joyful*. Wheaton, Illinois: Victor Books, 1974.

To order additional Bible Studies from Start2Finish, visit start2finish.org/bible-studies, call (888) 978-3850, or ask for them at your favorite Christian bookstore.

Also available for Kindle, Nook, & iBooks.

www.ingramcontent.com/pod-product-compliance
Lightning Source LLC
Chambersburg PA
CBHW062125040426
42337CB00044B/4261